JESUS DID WHAT FOR WHOM?

"I am the good shepherd; the good shepherd giveth his life for the sheep."

John 10:11

Moreno Dal Bello

JESUS DID WHAT FOR WHOM?

It is seldom taught otherwise, in what is perceived by most to be Christian institutions, that Jesus Christ went to the cross and laid down His precious life for every individual in all the world. It is also taught that the door to salvation has been swung open by Christ and it is now up to each individual to make the choice to enter in or not. **Such teaching alleges that the saved are a generation of choosers, not *"a chosen generation"* as the Scriptures clearly teach! (1 Peter 2:9).** The popular belief is that Christ did not actually *save* anyone on the cross, but that He merely made salvation *possible* for all. Potentially, salvation is possible for everyone living today if only *they* would make that one decision for Christ. This presents us with the possibility that if no one would *choose* Christ, then all of what He did on the cross would have been in vain. Doubtless it will come as a shock to those who have been taught nothing else, that this is all a manifestation of mans' imagination. The teachings that Christ died for every man—**universalism**—and that a man comes to God by his own **free will** choice, do *not* originate within the pages of God's Word but were popularized by a man named James Arminius. *"An early perpetrator of Arminianism and Humanism is 3rd century Pelagianism, which exalted the human will above that of the God of the Bible."* That is, though God has made salvation possible, He cannot save even one man unless that man chooses God by his own determination, by his free will. **In other words it is not that which God has Sovereignly decreed, but only that which man agrees to, which will occur.** The whole basis for such a teaching finds no ground in God's Word and does away with an All-Powerful Sovereign God Who **"...doeth according to His will in the army of heaven, and among the inhabitants of the earth..."** (Dan.4:35). Many Scriptures have been so twisted that they appear to say that Christ has indeed died for every man and that the onus is now on man to choose God and come to Him. This short pamphlet will teach otherwise. It will present the reader with irrefutable evidence and Biblical facts that show beyond a shadow of doubt that all such teaching is a God-defaming lie and that it does no justice whatsoever to Who Christ Jesus is and what Christ Jesus has done for the people for whom He laid down His life.

If salvation is conditioned on the sinner and his choice of God, how could man possibly do his part—accepting what has been done on his behalf—when Scripture states clearly that man is dead in sin and dead to God and incapable of coming to God in the prescribed manner? **"There is none that understandeth, there is none that seeketh after God. They are all gone out of the way, they are together become unprofitable; there is none that doeth good, no, not one"** (Rom.3:11,12); **"Wherefore, as by one man sin entered into the world, and death by sin; and so death passed upon all men, for that all have sinned"** (Rom.5:12). All those to whom God gives the power to become sons of God and to believe on His name are those **"Which were born, NOT of blood, NOR of the will of the flesh, NOR of the will of man, BUT OF GOD"** (Jn.1:13). **"Thy people shall be willing in the day of Thy power..."** (Ps.110:3). The Bible teaches that unless God draws a man to His Son, salvation is utterly impossible. Jesus says, **"No man CAN come to Me, except the Father which hath sent Me draw him: and I will raise him up at the last day"** (Jn.6:44). Most are taught that God indeed does draw the man, He enables the man to come to Him, but unless *man does the coming,* no salvation can take place. In other words, God has most certainly done His part in salvation but unless man does his, none can be saved. Such teaching is quite subtle, nevertheless it cannot hide the fact that it denies that what God has done is enough to save a sinner and that something more needs to be added, which in this case is man's 'free-will' decision. It makes saving faith a work rather than a Gift from God. **Coming to God is attributed to a free-will act on man's part rather than something which occurs only by the Grace, Mercy and Power of God.** This is man-centred humanistic 'theology' and not at all what the Word of God teaches. **"...the GIFT OF GOD is eternal life through Jesus our Lord"** (Rom.6:23). **SALVATION IS NOT BY FREE WILL BUT BY A FREE GIFT!** God's Word teaches that man, by nature (in his natural unsaved state), is without God and therefore without hope in this world (Eph.2:12). In answering His disciples' question as to who can be saved, Christ Jesus Himself said, **"With men this is IMPOSSIBLE; but with God all things are possible"** (Matt.19:26). This shows clearly that without God's intervention man is hopelessly lost in a whirlpool of sin and nothing within him, not free will nor zealous religious desire, can save him. In fact no man, by nature, even *seeks* God so how could man, of his own volition, come to God? **A MAN IS SAVED NOT BECAUSE HE HAS COME TO GOD BUT BECAUSE GOD HAS COME TO THE MAN.** God does not love a man because of the man's love-driven, free-will-fuelled choice of God, but a man loves God because God loved the man FIRST! (see 1 Jn.4:19). Put simply, if you have been taught and led to believe in a salvation conditioned on man doing something, **whether his doing it is attributed to God or not,** you have a gospel of works which cannot save (see Lk.18:9-14).

  A fact which has escaped the attention of those who have been wrongly taught that Jesus Christ died for every individual ever born and has made satisfaction for all their sins, is that if Christ has died for everyone and made atonement for all the sins of every individual, **would not this great atoning work also cover the sin which causes man's greatest impediment in coming to God, that of unbelief?** Popular 'christianity' teaches that God has done His part by providing a Savior, a High Priest who has made atonement for every sin of every individual ever born, and that the only thing that now needs to be done to make all this effective in a person's life, to make it real, is man coming to God, man choosing God. In light of this, would it not be reasonable to pose the following: Would not *every* man come to God if Jesus was the Propitiation, the Satisfaction for them all and paid the penalty for their every sin, **for the sin of unbelief would have also been done away with!** Otherwise we would have this situation: Jesus Christ has made atonement for every sin of every individual ever born, **including the sin of unbelief,** but hell is, nevertheless, full of people who died in unbelief, a sin that, along with man's other sins, was nailed to Christ's cross! One might answer,

'Yes, but you must remember that even though Christ died for the sin of selfishness, some Christians are, on occasion, selfish, so it is no problem to believe that Christ died for the sin of unbelief of every man, even though some of those men die in unbelief.' **This sounds quite reasonable if one does not understand what Christ accomplished on the cross.** Christ's death for the sins of His people does not mean that they will never again commit those sins, but that He has **paid the penalty in full** which those sins incur. The sin of unbelief is very different to other sins, for it is the only **unpardonable sin** and no man can be saved whilst an unbeliever. Therefore the sin of unbelief is one which the truly saved man can never again commit for he has received eternal life and eternal life means an eternal faith, a belief and reliance **solely** upon God for salvation—**a salvation which has eternally rescued a man from the sin and state of unbelief.**

      The death blow to the false teaching of universalism is this: God would be unjust to receive satisfactory payment for man's sins from Christ His Son and then demand that the sinner also make payment. If Christ has actually put away all the sins of everyone He died for, then there remains no further payment to be made. **"It is finished"!** (Jn.19:30) Christ said upon the cross and so **the matter is closed!** If all sin has been atoned for, would it not be right to conclude that the sin of unbelief has also been taken out of the way? **For what good would it have done and what sense would it have made for Christ to atone for every sin EXCEPT that ultimate and unpardonable sin which keeps a man out of heaven, the sin of unbelief?** If it is not in accord with Scripture to believe that the sin of unbelief was amongst those sins which were nailed to Christ's cross, then the sin of unbelief has not been done away with for **ANY** man, moreover, there is no atonement for it. The penalty it incurs has not been paid and therefore **no one can possibly come to God, via God's will or man's,** for the sin of unbelief reigns supreme, being untouched by the atoning blood of Christ. I am sure the reader can already see that the doctrines of universal atonement and free will contradict what the Word of God says.

One man has wisely put forward the following summary and we present it here for your examination. **Please note that each one of these points stand in opposition to the other two and therefore only one of the following scenarios can be right. They cannot co-exist. The other two are lies which are found only in false gospels and belief in them has not, and will not, save anyone.**

"The Father imposed His wrath due unto, and the Son underwent punishment for, either:

1. All the sins of all men.

2. All the sins of some men, or

3. Some of the sins of all men.

In which case it may be said:

a. That if the last be true, all men have some sins to answer for, and so, none are saved.

b. That if the second be true, then Christ, in their stead suffered for all the sins of all the elect in the whole world, and this is the truth.

c. But if the first be the case, why are not all men free from the punishment due unto their sins?

You answer, 'Because of unbelief.' I ask, 'Is this unbelief a sin, or is it not?' If it be, then Christ suffered the punishment due unto it, or He did not. If He did, why must that hinder them more than their other sins for which He died? If He did not, He did not die for all their sins!"

      If Jesus Christ has suffered the punishment for all the sins of every individual, which is what most people have been, and are being, taught in most so-called 'christian' denominations, would you think it fair for a Just and Holy God to again visit punishment upon those very same sins by sending people to hell for whom Christ has already paid the penalty? If you say, *'But Christ did not pay the penalty for the sins of those who die in unbelief,'* you make Christ's work upon the cross some great fiction where *something was done, but not really done* if it is not accepted and believed. **Quite clearly, its a case of the Arminian's savior being the savior you have when you haven't got a savior!** The following illustration shows clearly the nonsensical nature of such a teaching: if someone tells you that they have paid your electricity bill, then either they have paid it or not. They cannot say to you, *'If you accept what I have done then I have paid your bill.'* Either they have paid it, that is, handed over the money, made the transaction and the bill has been stamped PAID, or they are lying! This is in fact a perfect illustration, for the Bible says that the sins for which Christ has paid the penalty have all been NAILED to His Cross (Col.2:14), alluding to the middle eastern tradition which is even used in many western countries, of driving a nail through an account thus signifying payment/satisfaction made and that no further payment is required or necessary. How many times must one pay an electricity bill in order for the electric company to be satisfied? **What has *your* acceptance got to do with this transaction done on your behalf? *Your* acceptance is not that which validates (gives legal force to) the transaction, IT IS THE PAYMENT MADE WHICH CANCELS THE DEBT!** Is it not the sole business of the one who has paid the price and the one to whom the price was owing? The one who has had his bill paid is merely the beneficiary of what was done on his behalf. **How many times must God punish sin in order to be satisfied? Surely God's wrath towards the sin of those Christ suffered punishment for was exhausted on the cross. Surely God's method of dealing with sin was successful and absolutely fulfilled by Christ's blood shed on the cross, for this was the method God designated to deal with sin. This was God's perfect solution to mans' sin problem.**

Has not Christ suffered the penalty of all sins, including the sin of unbelief? **If so, how could anyone for whom Christ has suffered, possibly die in unbelief when the penalty for that very sin of unbelief has already been paid by the Lord Jesus?** Because of Christ's death there is no longer any penalty for unbelief awaiting those for whom He died, so how can anyone for whom He died possibly die in unbelief? Those who insist that, though Christ died for all the sins of all people, a person will still go to hell if they do not choose Him, must live with the fact that this blind theology leaves them to conclude that a man who dies in unbelief must pay the price for his sins that Christ has already paid and which has already appeased the Wrath of Almighty God, and for which God's Justice no longer makes any demands. **But what penalty can such a person be expected to pay when it has already been paid by Christ on the cross? Significantly, this would also mean that it is not Christ's death which makes the difference between saved and lost but each individual sinner's decision to accept Christ. Scripture refutes this: *"For who maketh thee to differ from another? And what hast thou that thou didst not receive?..."* (1Cor.4:7). In all things Christ Jesus must have the pre-eminence** (Col.1:18).

All this shows quite clearly that Christ has not put away the sins of every individual, but those sins alone which belonged to the elect of God. The Bible abounds with Scripture after Scripture telling us that God has elected a people from every nation, not just the Jewish nation, to be His people (Rev.5:9) and those are the very people for whom Christ has laid down His life: *"**Husbands, love your wives, even as Christ also loved the Church, and gave Himself for it**"* (Eph.5:25). The word *church* here means *'called out ones'*, called out of the world by God. Acts 3:25 spells it out plain and simple: *"**Ye are the children of the prophets, and of the covenant which God made with our fathers, saying unto Abraham, And in thy seed shall ALL THE KINDREDS OF THE EARTH be blessed**"* (see also Gen.12:3; 18:18; 22:18; 26:4; Ps.72:17). Galatians 3:8 also points out that people of every nation shall be saved: *"**And** *the Scripture, foreseeing that God would justify the heathen through faith, preached before the Gospel unto Abraham, saying, In thee shall ALL NATIONS BE BLESSED."* Election is not according to any man's works—including his accepting or believing—but according to the grace of God alone: *"Of His own will begat He us with the Word of Truth..."* (Js.1:18; see also Tit.3:7). These elect ones from every nation have been given the Perfect Righteousness of Christ and have had their sins imputed (charged) to His account. Christ has nailed to His cross every sin of every person God the Father has given to Him and they are the ones who shall be saved: *"All that the Father giveth Me SHALL come to me; and him that cometh to Me I will in no wise cast out"* (Jn.6:37). This is the only teaching concerning Christ's death which does justice to Him and glorifies the Son of God, for it shows that He has triumphed through the Cross, His death, for the shedding forth of His precious blood successfully accomplished atonement and redemption for all those He was sent to save. To believe anything else is to say that Christ failed in fulfilling that which He set out to do, and that contradicts the fact that Christ is God and Perfect and cannot fail in any endeavor He pursues: *"And Thou hast given Him power over all flesh, that He should give eternal life to AS MANY AS THOU HAST GIVEN HIM"* (not to as many as choose Him!) (Jn.17:2). It would be unscriptural, therefore wrong, to say that Christ has given eternal life to any apart from those whom God has given to Him. **So too, it would be equally wrong to conclude that Christ has died for any apart from those whom God has given Him.** It would also be wrong to say that all those whom God has given to His Son is every person ever born, for this would mean all are saved. All whom the Father has given to the Son have/will be given eternal life and not one will miss out, for they have been given by the Father to the Son and the Son has, in turn, died and established a Righteousness for all those to whom He now gives eternal life: *"All that the Father giveth me SHALL COME TO ME..."* (Jn.6:37); *"And you,* (believers) *being dead in your sins and the uncircumcision of your flesh, hath He quickened* (made alive) *together with Him,* *having forgiven you all trespasses; Blotting out the handwriting of ordinances that was against us, which was contrary to us, and took it out of the way, nailing it to His cross"* (Col.2:13,14). The elect are the chosen bride of Christ—chosen by the Father Himself. A man comes to God, not by his own 'free-will' decision, but only in the day of God's power, because God has given that one to Christ the Son to save. **GOD HAS CHOSEN A MAN, GOD HAS GIVEN THAT MAN TO CHRIST, AND CHRIST HAS DIED FOR THAT MAN.**

In order to know **who** Christ died for, that is, for whom He laid down His precious life as a sacrifice in order to fully and effectively atone for their sin, we must ask ourselves, *'What did Christ do on the Cross?'* **What Christ has done is something which cannot be separated from the doctrine which tells us *who* Christ actually died for.** What Christ has done lies at the very heart of the Gospel and if you have been taught incorrectly about what Christ has done on the cross, you cannot come to a proper biblical conclusion regarding who He has died for. **You have been taught a false gospel about another christ who cannot save.** The very name 'JESUS' means **"He will save His people from their sins"** (Matt.1:21). The Bible says that Christ is the Great High Priest of His people (Heb.4:14). The best study of the work of Jesus Christ as the High Priest of His people is found in the Letter to the Hebrews. **As in the Old Testament, so it is in the New.** God has appointed a Mediator between Himself and man. In the Old Testament it was between God and the nation of Israel, which was the **shadow** of the **substance** found in the New Testament. In the New Testament God has appointed His Son to be the Mediator between Himself and His chosen people, who come from every nation, tribe and language. **It is important to remember that the high priest's role as the mediatorial representative was to represent a specific group, or number, of people to God, and to represent God to that specific group/number of people.** The high priest did not do what he did for an unspecified or indeterminate number of people, upon whom depended the success of what he did. For those who are not convinced of this by Scripture alone, this writer has had it verified by an independent source, namely a Jewish rabbi who is not a Christian, that the Old Testament plainly teaches that the high priest did what he did for the people of God **exclusively**, and what he did was not dependant, or conditioned, on each individual's acceptance of what was done on their behalf, but that the success of the atoning sacrifice depended solely on what the high priest did under the direction of God. **Salvation is not conditioned on the sinner, for the sinner could never meet any of the conditions laid down by God.** The very fact that man needs a Savior, someone to save him, demonstrates clearly that there is nothing inherent in man that he can employ which will gain him acceptance with, or recommend himself to, God. How could any man come to God, freely choose Him by exercising his 'free will', when God Himself states that all are under sin and *"...there is none righteous, no, not one: There is none that understandeth, there is none that seeketh after God"* (Rom.3:10,11). No man, by nature, can come to God or even desire to seek the true God for all are under sin, they are dead in sin and dead to God and, by nature, do not understand the Way to God. Now please do not misconstrue what is being said here. There *are* conditions for salvation: **perfect obedience to God's law and perfect satisfaction of God's wrath towards sin.** It must be said, however, that simply because there are conditions to be met in order for a man to be saved, should not immediately lead us to conclude, as those of the Pelagian/Arminian persuasion would have us do, that those upon whom the conditions have been laid are in any way able to fulfill them. If this were the case, man would be justified in seeking salvation by his own efforts and salvation would be by the works of man and not by the grace and mercy of God. Where then would man's works have to begin and when would they end. When would the grace of God come into play? Where would one find Scripture to support such an abominable collaboration between man's works and God's grace? **The conditions of salvation are made known to show us that no ordinary man could possibly ever fulfill them and that we need to look to an EXTRAORDINARY Man to act on our** behalf. **They are designed, not to cause us to look to ourselves, but to turn to Him for Hope.**

In light of this, I am sure the reader will have no problem agreeing that no man can meet the conditions laid down by God for salvation: **perfect obedience to God's Law and perfect satisfaction for sins.** That is why, if any man was to be saved, he needed a Mediator, a Liaison, a High Priest. Not a high priest taken from among sinful men, but a high priest who was perfect and sinless, sent of God. Jesus Christ is the One Whom God appointed and whose Priesthood is forever (Heb.7:24). Christ needs not to repeat His sacrifice for the sins of His sheep yearly, as the Old Testament high priest did for the sins of Israel, because Christ's sacrifice was perfect (Heb.7:26,27). The Blood of Christ satisfied all the demands of God's Justice paying the penalty in full for all the sins of God's chosen ones. We learn from this that salvation is not achievable by any individual's efforts in obeying God's Law but is solely dependant on, and because of, the efforts and achievements of ONE MAN: Jesus Christ the Savior! **"...BY THE OBEDIENCE OF ONE shall many be made righteous"** (Rom.5:19); **"Be it known unto you therefore, men and brethren, that through this Man (Jesus)** *is preached unto you the forgiveness of sins:* **and BY HIM all that believe are justified from all things..."** (Acts 13:38,39); **"But God commendeth His love toward us, in that, while we were yet sinners, Christ died for us. Much more then, being now justified by His blood, we shall be SAVED FROM WRATH THROUGH HIM"** (Rom.5:8,9; see also 1Thess.1:10; 5:9). The Bible says we are fully reconciled to God by the death of His Son (Rom.5:10). **NO wrath remains for the sins for which Christ has suffered and died.** As one man wisely put it: **"Jesus Christ has drunk damnation dry"** for every sinner for whom He died.

The following is a vitally important study of: Jesus Christ the Savior:

a) WHY He is the Savior

b) WHOM He has saved

c) HOW He has accomplished salvation.

"*The Old Testament types* (examples or models) *supply incontrovertible evidence that the Gospel was no novel invention of New Testament times. When the risen Savior would make known to His disciples the meaning of His death, we read that,* **"Beginning at Moses and all the prophets, He expounded unto them in all the Scriptures the things concerning Himself"** *(Lk.24:27). So far from the evangel of the apostle's being any (absolutely) new thing, every element in it was revealed long centuries before their birth, not only in words, but in visible representations: there was both a wondrous anticipation of and preparation for the Gospel. Thus a reverent contemplation of the types supplies a blessed confirmation of faith, for they attest the Divine Authorship of both Testaments. Moreover, they stimulate adoration, even when we know a person, we enjoy looking at his picture; so here. It is Christ that is before us in them.*

The Divine origin of sacrifice is self-evident. Whoever would have dreamed of the device of offering animal sacrifices to God as a method of acceptable worship? That Abel should have **"brought of the firstlings of his flock and of the fat thereof"** *(Gen.4:4), can only be satisfactorily accounted for on the ground that he knew this was what God required from him. And this is precisely what the New Testament affirms: Hebrews 11:4 declares that it was:* **"by faith"** *that Abel offered his sacrifice, and Romans 10:17 says* **"faith cometh by hearing, and hearing by the word of God."** *Thus, Abel had received a revelation from God, and believing what he had "heard," acted accordingly. Moreover, the acceptance of Abel's sacrifice by a Divine testimony of approval (Gen.4:4), which, no doubt, was given by the descent of consuming fire from heaven—Leviticus 9:24; Judges 6:21; 1 Kings 18:38—intimate the same thing. That solemn testimony of reception would only have terrified the offerer, had he himself invented this mode of worship! 'The lightning shooting round the altar, and consuming the victim, would have conveyed the impression of an angry God: how, then, could they have apprehended by this means that they were reconciled? How could they have known without a*

Divine revelation that this consuming fire was a token of Divine acceptance?'

The great sacrifice of Christ was foreshadowed from the beginning. He Who predestinated the salvation of His elect, did also appoint the means thereto: the Lamb was **"foreordained before the foundation of the world"** *(1Pet.1:20). Then what memorial could be devised more opposite than that of animal sacrifices? By such a means was exemplified the death which had been denounced upon man's disobedience, and in the shedding of the victim's blood and the violent character of its death, was portrayed something of the awfulness of that death which was the* **"wages of sin"**. *At the same time a fit representation was also made of that death that was to be undergone by the Redeemer, and thus there was connected in one view the two cardinal facts in the history of men—the fall and recovery from it. The Old Testament sacrifices were a showing forth of the Lord's death till He came.*

It is both important and blessed to note that the Gospel-covenant was revealed by God immediately after the Fall. The promise that the woman's Seed should bruise the serpent's head (Gen.3:15) and the institution of the types (Gen.3:21), were to the very end that faith and hope might be preserved in what God had so graciously purposed. God did not leave even our first parents in ignorance of His merciful designs, but made known the nature of His eternal counsels. Soon after, a further revelation was made unto Cain and Abel, and still later to others. The infinite wisdom of God so contrived the types that they might in the most intelligible manner (that material things can describe spiritual) signify the Redeemer, and life and salvation through Him. From the time of the fall, there has been but one way open to Heaven, and that was through Christ; and all believers, before and under the law, hoped for pardon of sin and salvation through Him. In hopes of that pardon and salvation they observed the typical services." **These services were the types and shadows of the Savior that was to come. They represented what He would do and what would be done through Him.**

"That the Old Testament saints perceived something at least of the mystical and spiritual meaning of the types is clear from a number of passages; that they had a much clearer and fuller apprehension of them than is commonly supposed, is the writer's firm conviction. The Lord Jesus declared that **"Abraham rejoiced to see My day: and he saw, and was glad"** (Jn.8:56) Hebrews 11:13 tells us that the patriarchs confessed themselves to be **"strangers and pilgrims on the earth,"** which shows they knew that their true **"inheritance"** was in Heaven; while Hebrews 11:14, 16 expressly states they sought and desired **"an heavenly"** country. Job said, **"I know that my Redeemer liveth"** (19:25), and the Hebrew word there for "Redeemer" signifies one who is a redeemer by right of affinity or kinship—not only a Redeemer in act, but in office." Christ says: **"I am the Good Shepherd, and know My sheep, and am known of Mine....and I lay down My life for the sheep"** (Jn. 10:14,15). The Scriptures also say that Christ **"...was made like unto His brethren..."** (Heb. 2:17). Hebrews 2:11 says **"...He is not ashamed to call them** (those that are sanctified) **brethren."** Christ the Savior did not lay down His life for anyone other than His sheep whom He foreknew and with whom He had affinity and kinship, for they had been given Him by the Father and were His (see Jn. 6:37 & Jn. 17:9,10). Those for whom He would die are called **"...His seed..."** (Isa. 53:10). Christ did not die for anyone other than His sheep, for it is with them that He has affinity, it is with them He is related, for He was made like unto THEM. "David acknowledged, **"my flesh longeth for Thee...to see Thy power and Thy glory, so as I have seen Thee in the sanctuary"** (Psa.63:2), that Is (David had seen His Lord), by means of the figures and shadows of the vessels of the tabernacle and the Levitical services and sacrifices.

"First the blade, then the ear and then the full corn in the ear" (Mk.4:28) enunciates one of the principles of Divine work in everything, the types not excepted. The further we proceed, the profounder their meaning, and the fuller their detail. In the Divine clothing of our first parents with **"coats of skins"** (Gen.3:21), there were illustrated the facts that: fallen man needed an external covering to fit him to stand before God; that he could not produce this by his own labors; that the life of an innocent victim must be taken, in order to provide a suitable covering for him; that God Himself must provide it. In the offering of Abel and God's acceptance of the same (Gen.4:4), we learn that God can only regard any sinner with favor by virtue of his acceptance in Christ. The Divine origin of sacrifices is again intimated in that before flesh was eaten by man, the distinction between clean and unclean animals was quite familiar (Gen.8:20). The power of an accepted sacrifice to remove the Divine curse was plainly signified in Genesis 8:21. The principle of substitution was strikingly manifested in Genesis 22:13." **It was the Substitutionary sacrifice of Christ which removed the curse from those for whom He died, for He was made a curse for them (Gal.3:13).**

"What may be termed the first great sacrifice was the **"Passover,"** recorded in Exodus 12. There we behold the efficacy of the lamb's precious blood to deliver those sheltering beneath it from that judgement of God which their sins deserved. What virtue, an infidel might ask, had the blood of a poor animal to secure the life of Israel's first-born from the sword of a mighty and invisible angel? Was the blood on the door a necessary mark for the angel, because he had not understanding enough to distinguish between the houses of Egyptians and Israelites? Could not God have signified His pleasure to the angel without such a mark as that? The answer to these, and all such questions is, God's design was to furnish a type of Christ, and instruct the faith of His people in things to come.

The following is a bare outline of the point in the Passover-type which may be profitably studied by the reader. First, Divine judgement was pronounced: **"all the firstborn [the representative of the family] in [not of] the land of Egypt shall die"** (Ex.11:5). Second, GOD **"put a difference between the Egyptians and Israel"** so that not one of His own people were hurt (Ex.11:7 cf. 1 Cor. 4:7; Jn. 3:27)." **(God is the One Who makes the difference between saved and lost, between death and life, not a sinner's free will choice).** "Third, not by Israel's choice or Moses' recommendation, but BY DIVINE APPOINTMENT every

Israelitish household was to take an unblemished lamb, kill it, and apply its blood to the outside of his house (Ex.12:3-7). Fourth, the Divine promise was, **"when I see the blood, I will pass over you"** (Ex.12:13). Fifth, the angel entered not such houses, for DEATH HAD ALREADY DONE ITS WORK THERE—a substitute had been slain. Here is redemption; deliverance from judgement." **Here is exactly what we have informed the reader about in earlier pages, here is the work of Jesus Christ as presented in the Old Testament. The Substitute was slain for a particular group of people and those people were directly related to Him through God's appointment and not something initiated by their choice.**

"At Sinai God made known His will much more fully respecting the sacrifices which He required. A great deal of instruction therein is to be found in the first seven chapters of Leviticus, into most of which we cannot now enter: much deeply important teaching is to be found therein in a typical form. The Levitical sacrifices emphasized the enormity of sin and the punishment which must be visited upon it, as well as set forth the dependence of the forgiving grace of God on an expiatory offering. Under the Mosaic economy an elaborate system was developed to show that in many ways man offends God and is worthy of death. The sacrifices vividly evidenced the fact that the Divine punishment incurred was inevitable, yet that that PUNISHMENT COULD BE BORNE BY A SUBSTITUTE, and ON THAT GROUND the offender could be restored to favor. The principal thing they were designed to exhibit was the indispensable necessity of atonement by vicarious expiation (the death of a Substitute): the one great truth they illustrated was that God could not sacrifice His holiness to His love." **For God to remain Just and be the Justifier of sinners, His Law had to be obeyed perfectly and His wrath had to be satisfied, thus establishing a perfect Righteousness.**

"That the Mosaic sacrifices all pointed forward to Christ and had their end in Him, was evidenced by the fact that very soon after He had come and shed His blood, God caused the shadows to pass away. Within a very few years the temple was destroyed, and with it all the Jewish sacrifices ceased. And though a century or two later Julian the Apostate gave the Jews permission to build their temple, and that for the very purpose of restoring the ancient rites, yet God from Heaven blasted all their attempts in a miraculous and extraordinary manner.

The Levitical sacrifices made clear to men the ground on which the Divine pardon could be obtained. It was not an act of absolute mercy, nor was it bestowed on the sole condition of penitence, but on the consideration of something quite distinct from both. **"And it shall be, when he shall be guilty in one of these things, that he shall confess that he hath sinned in that thing. And he shall bring his trespass offering unto the Lord for his sin...and the priest shall make an atonement for him concerning his sin...and it shall be forgiven him"** (Lev.5:5,6,10). If we compare these verses with Leviticus 17:11, which informs us that **"it is the blood which maketh an atonement for the soul,"** then the proof is conclusive that the sacrifice presented by the offender was the appointed means of obtaining forgiveness for his transgression.

The burnt offering (Lev.1) and the sin offering (Lev.4) claim particular attention, for not only were they the most important sacrifices of the Levitical dispensation (as Psalm 40:6 intimates), but they represented the sufferings of our great High Priest under two distinct aspects. The burnt offering principally shows Christ as He was to God, the sin offering as He is to men. In both He was represented as a SIN-BEARER, for in both of these sacrifices TRANSFER WAS MADE OF SIN by the priest laying his hand on the head of the victim (Lev.1:4; 4:4); in both the victim's blood was shed and sprinkled (Lev.1:5; 4:4-6); in both atonement was made for sin (1:4; 4:20); and both were burnt, either wholly or in part upon the altar (1:9; 4:9,10). These points of union were sufficiently close to show that they corresponded in representing the sacrifice offered by our High Priest on the cross." **We see in all this that the sins of a particular people were transferred to the substitute and the sins of those people were the only ones dealt with. It was their sins alone which were borne by the sin-bearer! Remember that all this was a shadow of the** substance—what Christ the Savior would do for His people. Christ was the **SIN-BEARER! A particular and exclusive group of people, namely God's elect, have had their sins taken, or borne, by Christ, the bearer of their sins, and nailed to His cross. The transferral of their sin is complete and payment has been made.**

"But there were also distinctive differences between them (the burnt offering and the sin offering) *of a character sufficiently marked to show that they represented Christ's sacrifice under different aspects. Thus, the burnt offering was voluntary (Lev.1:2,3), the sin offering compulsory (Lev.4:2,3). The burnt offering was flayed, cut into pieces, and the inwards and legs washed in water; but none of these things were required of the sin offering. The blood of the burnt offering was merely sprinkled round about upon the altar (1:1), but the blood of the sin offering was put upon the horns of the altar, sprinkled seven times before the Lord, before the veil of the sanctuary, and poured out at the bottom of the altar of burnt offering (4:6,7). Other differences we now pass over, desiring to direct attention merely to the first one mentioned.*

The voluntariness of Christ's death is clearly brought out in Psalm 40:7,8 and Ephesians 5:25; John 10:17,18 also shows He freely laid down His life for His sheep. But, when in the councils of eternity ratified by the everlasting covenant **"ordered in all things and sure,"** *Christ had undertaken to be our Surety, then what was before purely free and voluntary became in a sense compulsory. Just as when God binds Himself by oath, He is obliged to fulfill His word, so Christ once He had bound Himself to stand in His peoples' place and stead, was no longer free—though, not that He wished to be free. Just as the type was bound with cords* **"unto the horns of the altar"** *(Ps.118:27), so Christ was held fast to the Cross not only by love to His people, which floods could not quench, but by His own eternal covenant-engagement.*

The substitution of Christ in the sinner's place was most distinctly shown in the types, particularly in the sin offering. Before the animal was slaughtered, the sacrificing priest laid his hand upon its head (Lev.4:3,4). That act *represented THE TRANSFERRING OF SIN FROM THE TRANSGRESSOR TO THE VICTIM (Lev.16:21): it identified the one with the other. <u>It showed the substitution of the victim for the offender, and declared by a visible sign that it bare his sins and endured his death-penalty."</u>* **"For He hath made Him to be sin for us, who knew no sin; that we might be made the righteousness of God in Him"** (2Cor.5:21). **There was a specific transgressor whose sins were transferred to a specific victim.** *"In this way was the solemn yet blessed truth of imputation foreshadowed. It was because God transferred to Christ the guilt of His elect, constituting Him "sin for us," (sin-bearer) that the sword of Divine justice smote Him as He bare our sins in His own body on (or "to") the tree."* **By this we see clearly that Christ's atoning death cannot be separated from His act of Substitution, nor can it be separated from the act of transferring to Him the sins of those for whom He was a Substitute, and transferring His perfect Righteousness to them. All this hinged, not on man's acceptance, but on God accepting what Christ had done.**

"*The most important of all the types is that which is found in Leviticus 16: the appointed ritual for the great day of atonement. The type of Leviticus 16 goes much farther than does the one in Exodus 12: the Passover illustrated the redemptive character of Christ's sacrifice; that of Leviticus 16 its propitiatory* (satisfactory) *nature. In Exodus 12 we see the blood sheltering from judgement those who are under it; in the early chapters of Leviticus, we see the power of the blood restoring to communion the penitent transgressor; but in Leviticus 16 we behold the blood opening a way into the very presence of God, entitling the penitent and believing worshipper to come with boldness unto His very Throne.*

By a careful comparison of Deuteronomy 27 and Leviticus 16 we may discover how the law was, and still is, a **"schoolmaster"** *unto Christ (Gal.3:24). In the former chapter, we see that the law demanded implicit and complete obedience to its demands (v.10); and how that the Levites pronounced with* **"a loud voice"** *a curse on the transgressor of it (vv.14,15). That curse was repeated twelve times,* according to the number of Israel's tribes, and on each pronouncement thereof **"all the people"** were required to say **"Amen"**: the final word being **"Cursed be he that confirmeth not all the words of this law to do them"** (v.26)—cf. Gal. 3:10. The law required sinless perfection under the penalty of eternal damnation, and thus it revealed the imperative need of an atonement. While in Leviticus 16 we see how that law by its great sin-offering, with its blood of atonement, pointed forward to Christ.

    The sacrificial system of Judaism reached its climax on the great day of atonement. As the ark was the chief object in the tabernacle, so the annual Day of propitiation was the chief one in Israel's religious calendar. On that auspicious occasion the high priest divested himself of his robes of **"glory and beauty"** (Ex.28), and put on **"the holy linen"** garments (Lev.16:4). The spotless white in which he was clothed spoke of the perfect righteousness of Christ, which, tested as it was both by man (Jn. 8:46) and Satan (John 14:30), and then passing through the infinitely searching scrutiny of God under the fiery trial of the cross, insured the Divine acceptance of that satisfaction which He made to God on behalf of His people.

    Two young goats were selected **"for a sin-offering;"** though there were two animals, it was but one offering. Two goats were selected in order that a fuller representation might be given: the one being designed more expressly to exhibit the means the other the effect of the atonement. They were brought and presented together before the Lord (v.7), the Lord determining by lot which of them was to be slain. The other animal stood by and was atoned for (Hebrew of verse 10) by the dying victim, and then BORE AWAY THE SINS laid upon it into the land of eternal forgetfulness (vv.21,22): a blessed figure of that remission of our sins when we believe on the Lord Jesus Christ unto salvation.

    Passing by what was done with the bullock, we confine our attention to the two goats. After the one had been killed, the high priest took its blood within the veil and sprinkled it upon the mercy-seat not once, but seven times "before" Him to provide a perfect standing ground for His people. The antitype of this is seen in Hebrews 9:12, **"But by His own blood He entered in once into the holy place, having obtained eternal redemption"** *(Heb.9:12).* The consequence of this is that **"Having therefore, brethren, boldness to enter into the holiest by the blood of Jesus, by a new and living way which He hath consecrated for us"** *(Heb.10:19,20).*

After the high priest has finished his work inside the sanctuary, we are told, **"he shall bring the live goat, and Aaron shall lay both his hands upon the head of the live goat and confess over him all the iniquities of the children of Israel...and shall send him away by the hand of a fit man into the wilderness: and the goat shall BEAR UPON HIM ALL THEIR INIQUITIES unto a land not inhabited"** *(vv.20-22).* That was a continuation and completion of the ceremony concerning the sin-offering, so that this symbolic transfer of their sins to the head of the scapegoat, which bore them away, plainly signified that the atonement effected by the sacrifice of the first goat was <u>the complete removal of all their trangressions from before the face of God.</u>" **From this it is made clear that Christ died for those predetermined to be His people according to the grace and purpose of God. As Christ the Lamb was slain before the world began, so too, those for whom the Lamb was slain were all chosen by grace before the foundation of the world.**

"And Aaron shall come into the tabernacle of the congregation, and shall put off the linen garments, which he put on when he went into the holy place, and shall leave them there" *(Lev.16:23).* "Why? To denote that his work was finished. The blessed antitype of this we see in Luke 24:12: on the resurrection morning, those who came to Christ's empty sepulchre **"beheld the linen clothes"** lying there, a token that He was risen from the dead, and so of atonement completed, and accepted by God.

One other important feature in the types, often overlooked, claims our notice, namely, the burning of the victim's body on the altar *(Lev.1:10 etc.).* The animal was first slain as a just judgement for the sin which had been transferred to it by the laying on its head of the hand of the offerer; and then, after guilt had been borne, its flesh was laid on the altar and burned, and went up with acceptance unto God, a **"sweet smelling savor"** (Eph.5:2). In this was represented the glorious truth that, not only was Christ our sin-bearer, but that He is also our righteousness before God (Jer.23:6; 2Cor.5:21). We are identified with Him not only in His death for us, but also in the fragrance of it before God.

In Numbers 19 there is yet another most important type upon which we can only now say a few words. In it we see how the death of Christ has made full provision for those defilements which His people contract while passing through this evil world. In it too we behold again the steady progress in the types, and the deeper instruction which God gave to Israel from time to time. They were yet in the land of Pharaoh when the Passover was instituted: the doom of Egypt and their own deliverance therefrom were the thoughts then presented to their souls. Later, they were brought nigh to God, Himself tabernacling in their midst, and in Leviticus 16 they are shown the high demands of His Holiness. Now in Numbers 19, they are taught that even the unavoidable contact with death (the world lying in the Wicked one) defiles. But God has provided cleansing from it.

We call attention to one other deeply important value of the types and the use to which they may be put: they furnish an infallible rule by which can be tested any man's (our own included) interpretation of the New Testament Scriptures concerning the Atonement! He who denies the penal and vicarious nature of Christ's death, repudiates the clear testimony of the types; he who sets aside the efficacy of His sacrifice by reducing it to a merely 'making possible' the salvation does likewise, FOR THE TYPES KNOW NOTHING OF AN INEFFECTUAL SACRIFICE. So too in them we see plainly the limitation of God's love to His elect people, for no lamb was provided for the Egyptians, nor did Aaron make any atonement for the sins of the Midianites and Ammonites!" **So too, Christ's Substitutionary death was not on the behalf of the non-elect. It was not for those who were not among God's chosen ones whom He had given to Christ to die for, but only, and exclusively, for those**

elected by God to be His sheep, His children and the sole benefactors of Christ's work of salvation.

Finally, we deal with the passage of Scripture to which those who have been falsely taught about Christ and His death turn to in support of the teaching that Christ has laid down His life for all.

"There is one passage more than any other which is appealed to by those who believe in universal redemption, and which at first sight appears to teach that Christ died for the whole human race. We have therefore decided to give it a detailed examination and exposition.

"And He is the propitiation for our sins: and not for ours only, but also for the sins of the whole world" *(1 Jn.2:2). This is the passage which, apparently, most favors the Arminian view of the Atonement, yet if it be considered attentively it will be seen that it does so only in appearance, and not in reality. Below we offer a number of conclusive proofs to show that this verse does not teach that Christ has propitiated* (satisfied) *God on behalf of all the sins of all men.*

In the first place, the fact that this verse opens with **"and"** *necessarily links it with what has gone on before. We, therefore, give a literal word for word translation of 1 John 2:1 from Bagster's Interlinear:* **"Little children my, these things I write to you, that ye may not sin; and if anyone should sin, a paraclete we have with the Father, Jesus Christ (the) righteous".** *It will thus be seen that the apostle John is here writing to and about the saints of God. His immediate purpose was two-fold: first, to communicate a message that would keep God's children from sinning; second, to supply comfort and assurance to those who might sin, and, in consequence, be cast down and fearful that the issue would prove fatal. He, therefore, makes known to them the provision which God has made for just such an emergency. This we find at the end of verse 1 and throughout verse 2. The ground of comfort is twofold: let the downcast and repentant believer (1Jn.1:9) be assured that, first, he has an* **"Advocate with the Father"**; *second, that this Advocate is* **"the propitiation for our sins"**. *Now believers only may take comfort from this, for they alone have an* **"Advocate"**, *for them alone is Christ the propitiation, as is* *proven by linking the Propitiation ("and") with "the Advocate"!*

In the second place, if other passages in the New Testament which speak of "propitiation" be compared with 1 John 2:2, it will be found that it is strictly limited in its scope. For example, in Romans 3:25 we read that God set forth Christ **"a propitiation through faith in His blood"**. If Christ is a propitiation **"through faith"**, then He is not a **"propitiation"** to those who have no faith! Again, in Hebrews 2:17 we read, **"To make propitiation for the sins of the people."** *(Heb.2:17, R.V.)."* **This shows us that what Christ did on the cross could not possibly have been for those who would not believe in Him, but only for those who would be granted faith to believe in Him.**

"In the third place, who are meant when John says, **"He is the propitiation for our sins"**? We answer, Jewish believers. And a part of the proof on which we base this assertion we now submit to the careful attention of the reader.

In Galatians 2:9 we are told that John, together with James and Cephas, were apostles **"unto the circumcision"** (i.e. Israel). In keeping with this, the Epistle of James is addressed to **"the twelve tribes, which are scattered abroad"** (1:1). So, the first Epistle of Peter is addressed to **"the elect who are sojourners of the dispersion"** (1Pet.1:1, R.V.). And John is also writing to saved Jews.

Some of the evidences that John is writing to saved Jews are as follows. (a) In the opening verse he says of Christ, **"Which we have seen with our eyes....and our hands have handled"**. How impossible it would have been for the apostle Paul to have commenced any of his epistles to Gentile saints with such language!

(b) **"Brethren, I write no knew commandment unto you, but an old commandment which ye had from the beginning"** (1 Jn. 2:7). The **"beginning"** here referred to is the beginning of the public manifestation of Christ-in proof compare 1:1; 2:13, etc. Now these believers the apostle tells us, had the **"old commandment"** from the beginning. This was true of Jewish believers, but it was not true of Gentile believers.

(c) **"I write unto you fathers, because ye have known Him from the beginning"** (2:13). Here, again, it is evident that it is Jewish believers that are in view.

(d) **"Little children, it is the last time: and as ye have heard that Antichrist shall come, even now are there many antichrists; whereby we know that it is the last time. They went out from us, but they were not of us"** (2:18,19).

These brethren to whom John wrote had **"heard"** from Christ Himself that Antichrist should come (see Matt. 24). The **"many antichrists"** whom John declares **"went out from us"** were all Jews, for during the first century none but a Jew posed as the Messiah. Therefore, when John says **"He is the propitiation for our sins"** he can only mean for the sins of Jewish believers. (It is true that many things in John's Epistle apply equally to believing Jews and believing Gentiles. Christ is the Advocate of the one, as much as of the other. The same may be said of many things in the Epistle of James which is also a catholic (universal), or general epistle, though expressly addressed to the twelve tribes scattered abroad).

In the fourth place, when John added, **"And not for ours only, but also for the whole world"**, he signified that Christ was the propitiation for the sins of Gentile believers too, for, as previously shown, **"the world"** is a term contrasted from Israel. This interpretation is unequivocally established by a careful comparison of 1 John 2:2 with John 11:51,52, which is a strictly parallel passage: **"And this spake he not of himself: but being high priest that year, he prophesied that Jesus should die for that nation; And not for that nation only, but that also he should gather together in one the children of God that were scattered abroad"**. Here Caiaphas, under inspiration, made known for whom Jesus should "die". Notice now the correspondency of his prophecy with this declaration of John's:

"He is the propitiation for our (believing Israelites) sins."

"He prophesied that Jesus should die for that nation."

"And not for ours only." - That is, Gentile believers scattered throughout the earth.

"He should gather together in one of the children of God that were scattered abroad."

In the fifth place, the above interpretation is confirmed by the fact that no other is consistent or intelligible. If the **"whole world"** signifies the whole human race, then the first clause and the **"also"** in the second clause are absolutely meaningless. If Christ is the propitiation for every-body, it would be idle tautology to say, first, 'He is the propitiation for our sins and also for everybody.' There could be no 'also' if He is the propitiation for the entire human family. Had the apostle meant to affirm that Christ is a universal propitiation he had omitted the first clause of verse 2, and simply said, 'He is the propitiation for the sins of the whole world.' Confirmatory of 'not for ours (Jewish believers) only, but also for the whole world' - Gentile believers, too; compare John 10:16; 17:20.

In the sixth place, our definition of 'the whole world' is in perfect accord with other passages in the New Testament. For example: **"Whereof ye heard before in the word of the truth of the Gospel; which is come unto you, as it is in all the world"** (Col.1:5,6). Does 'all the world' here mean, absolutely and unqualifiedly, all mankind? Had all the human family heard the Gospel? No; the apostle's obvious meaning is that, the Gospel, instead of being confined to the land of Judea, had gone abroad, without restraint, into Gentile lands. So in Romans 1:8: **"First, I thank my God through Jesus Christ for you all, that your faith is spoken of throughout the whole world"**. The apostle is here referring to the faith of these Roman saints being spoken of in a way of commendation. But certainly all mankind did not so speak of their faith! It was the whole world of believers that he was referring to! In Revelation 12:9 we read of Satan **"which deceiveth the whole world"**. But again this expression cannot be *understood as a universal one, for Matthew 24:24 tell us that Satan does not and cannot 'deceive' God's elect. Here it is 'the whole world' of unbelievers.*

In the seventh place, to insist that 'the whole world' in 1 John 2:2 signifies the entire human race is to undermine the very foundations of our faith. If Christ is the propitiation for those that are lost equally as much as for those that are saved, then what assurance have we that believers too may not be lost? If Christ is the propitiation for those now in hell, what guarantee have I that I may not end in hell? The blood-shedding of the Incarnate Son of God is the only thing which can keep any one out of hell, and if many for whom that precious blood made propitiation are now in the awful place of the damned, then may not that blood prove inefficacious for me! Away with such a God-dishonoring thought." **The blood of Christ is that which makes the difference between saved and lost. Any teaching that denies this, that places emphasis on man's decision to accept what Christ has done, thus making IT the difference between saved and lost, is satanic to the very core.**

"However men may quibble and wrest the Scriptures, one thing is certain: The Atonement is no failure. God will not allow that precious and costly sacrifice to fail in accomplishing, completely, that which it was designed to effect. Not a drop of that holy blood was shed in vain. In the last great Day there shall stand forth no disappointed and defeated Savior, but One Who **"shall see of the travail of His soul and be satisfied"** *(Isa.53:11). These are not our words, but the infallible assertion of Him who declares,* **"My counsel shall stand, and I will do all My pleasure"** *(Isa.64:10). Upon this impregnable rock we take our stand. Let others rest on the sands of human speculation and twentieth-century theorizing if they wish. That is their business. But to God they will yet have to render an account. For our part we had rather be railed at as a narrow-minded, out-of-date (people), than be found repudiating God's Truth by reducing the Divinely-efficacious atonement to a mere fiction."*

It has been wisely said that *'Christianity is Christ'* and this is precisely what it is. To believe (put your trust) in Jesus one must know Him and there is no place where the True Christ is revealed other than in God's only Gospel: *"And this is life eternal, that they might know Thee the only True God, and Jesus Christ, Whom Thou hast sent"* (Jn.17:3). To believe in Christ is to know Him: **to know and believe in Who He is and to know and believe in what He has done for the sinner.** Christ did not die for everyone as so many believe. For if He did, then salvation would not be solely dependant on Him and what He has done, but would rely on each individual's *acceptance* of what He has done. It would depend on man choosing Him rather than on God having Sovereignly chosen who would become His children. **The Sacrifice Jesus Christ made to God on the behalf of all whom God had given Him is something which God, not man, had to accept in order to make what Christ did acceptable AND effectual.** Mans' part in salvation, the Bible says, is purely as a receiver, a receptacle. The saved man is referred to as **a vessel of mercy** (Rom.9:23). Just as a bottle plays no part in producing its contents, so too, the Christian has played no part in his salvation, for this is solely the role of God and His Son. Even mans' receiving is a result of God's blessing and the faith with which the true Christian believes does not spring from within, but is a gift from God. **Christ did something on the cross and what HE did actually saved those for whom He did it from the penalty and punishment that their sin had incurred.** Everyone for whom He laid Himself down as a Sacrifice has, and will, benefit eternally from what He has done. To say that what Christ has done has failed in any way to save even one sinner for whom He did it, or that our own personal obedience must be added to what Christ has done to ensure salvation, is to deny Him as the COMPLETE Savior. Some might ask, *'But surely there must be something we have to do in order to gain, or at the very least maintain, salvation?'* The response according to biblical reasoning is, **'WHY? Why must we do anything, when Christ Himself has done EVERYTHING to gain, maintain and secure the salvation of all those for whom He died?'**

Take these important teachings seriously. Examine the Bible and by all means test what you have just read by the Scriptures. Tell your pastor of these things and ask for his comment. It is incumbent upon you to thoroughly examine his response by the Holy Scriptures in the proper and biblical manner. Do not do yourself a disservice and injustice by simply casting into the fire what you have read here upon a mere word or two of contempt uttered by one you have come to respect as a 'man of God'. Be honest with yourself. Do not allow yourself to be deceived and influenced by bias and prejudice. There is no salvation in any gospel other than God's ONLY Gospel. **Remember that the true believer has nothing to fear from God's Truth, it is only those who do not have a love for the Truth who greatly fear it and flee from it. Believe the Gospel and you will be saved!**

FOR WHOM DID CHRIST PRAY?

"As Thou hast given Him power over all flesh, that He should give eternal life to as many as Thou hast given Him" (John 17:2). For whom else did Christ die but for those God gave to Him? And who could say that anyone from that group of people entrusted to Christ was not elected before the foundation of the world? Do you believe that Christ died for anyone whom God did not first give unto His Son? Do you think Christ died for those whom He did not pray for? "I have manifested Thy name unto the men which Thou gavest Me out of the world: Thine they were, and Thou gavest them Me....I pray for them: I pray not for the world, but for them which Thou hast given Me; for they are Thine....Neither pray I for these alone, but for them also which shall believe on Me through their word" (John 17:6,9,20). The Lord Jesus here states that He has revealed the Father only to those whom God gave unto Him out of the world. Jesus states quite clearly that He prays NOT for the world, those whom God DID NOT give unto Him, but exclusively for those whom God gave to Him. In saying this Christ makes a clear and distinct difference between those He prayed for and those He did not. Between those God gave to Him and those He did not. Christ adds that He did not pray only for those there with Him but also for all those who would believe on Him through their word. Obviously these who would believe were also given unto Christ by the Father out of the world. Do you think Christ died for the people He did pray for and/or those for whom He did not pray? The Lord Jesus only aligns Himself with those people who are the Father's, "And all Mine are Thine, and Thine are Mine; and I am glorified in them" (John 17:10). In other words Christ's people are God's people. And, God's people are the ones He chose before the foundation of the world according to the good pleasure of His will, "According as He hath chosen us in Him before the foundation of the world..." (Ephesians 1:4). Christ did not say that the Father gave unto Him everyone in the world but that those He did give unto Him wereout of the world. Now these are God's people, God's chosen. He chose them before the foundation of the world and entrusted everyone of them to His Son the Lord Jesus Christ. Those the Father did not give unto His Son are those whom He did not choose out of the world. Christ did not say that He prayed for the world but only for those God gave to Him out of the world. The distinct air of separation and distinction and exclusivity is quite evident.

Now how could anyone in their right mind think that Christ prayed for the world? Moreover, how could anyone possibly believe after reading these very words of Jesus the Savior that Christ died for everybody, for the world, those whom God gave to Him out of the world and for those He did not! To include both groups is to go against the grain of the entire tenth chapter of John, indeed the whole of Scripture. It is quite evident from Scripture that God did not love the people He did not give to His Son for if He did why did He not entrust them also to His Son? Why did He not call them out of the world? Does God favor some He loves above others? And if Christ loved them, indeed would die for them, why then did He not pray for them? Does anyone dare say that Christ did not exclusively pray for those God gave to Him out of the world? Of course not. Christ said it Himself, "I PRAY FOR THEM: I PRAY NOT FOR THE WORLD..." (John 17:9). Then how can anyone believe that Christ died for those He did not pray for? In essence Christ was saying here that which He said earlier in the Gospel of John, "...I lay down My life for the sheep" (John 10:15 see also verse 16). Now, does anyone believe that Christ prayed for anyone but the sheep? In light of this does anyone dare say that Christ died for those for whom He did not pray? For those who were not of His sheep? Is anyone that ignorant of the glaringly obvious? That Christ died, that He laid down His life, as the Substitutionary Sacrifice exclusively for those He prayed, for His sheep? The same ones whom God chose out of the world and entrusted to His Son? One needs to pause here for a moment and ask oneself the question, 'Why did God take these people out of the world and give them to His Son.' What does Jesus say He did in John's tenth chapter? Christ says clearly that He prayed for those people. Now who else could these people be but those very same people Christ died for whom He refers to as His sheep, the very same ones He prayed for? How then can anyone say that Christ died for those for whom He did not pray? For those God did not give to Him out of the world? For those whom Christ does not call His sheep? Who are these ones for whom Christ did not pray? Those who are of the world; the ones whom God did not take out of the world and entrust to Christ. These are the ones who are not among the chosen of God. These are of the world, these are the goats NOT THE SHEEP! (see Matthew 25:32-34,41). God did not choose them out of the world, He did not give them unto His Son which is why Christ did not love them, pray for them or die for them. They were not given unto Him for they were not chosen. Christ prayed for the people He would die for, and He died for the people He prayed for, the people God gave to Him. To say otherwise is to show one's ignorance of the Scriptures and therefore of God. If you do not have a problem with Christ praying ONLY for the people God gave Him, then you should not have a problem with Christ dying EXCLUSIVELY for those God gave Him. In writing to believers, John said, "Herein is love, not that we loved God, but that He loved us, and sent His Son to be the Propitiation for OUR sins" (1 John 4:10). The apostle Paul in His letter to the believers at Ephesus wrote, "Husbands, love your wives, even as Christ also loved THE CHURCH, AND GAVE HIMSELF FOR IT" (Ephesians 5:25). Who are those who make up the Church of Christ Jesus? They are the called out ones. Those God gave to Jesus are the people God loved, the ones He chose, called, out of the world. The same ones Christ loved, prayed for and died for. Just as Christ did not pray for the world, those who were not given to Him by the Father are not the people Christ died for. Christ prayed for those He would die for and He died for those whom He prayed for because those are the ones God chose from before the foundation of the world and gave unto His beloved Son. And, according to 1 John 4:10, these are the ones God sent His Son to the earth to die for, to be the Satisfaction for their sins.

Please Contact:

morenodalbello@yahoo.com.au

Please Visit:

www.godsonlygospel.com

Made in the USA
Monee, IL
03 May 2026